Explore
AFRICA

Bobbie Kalman & Rebecca Sjonger

Crabtree Publishing Company

www.crabtreebooks.com

Created by Bobbie Kalman

Dedicated by Bobbie Kalman
To Sister Delphine Nebie and Sister Elisabeth Badini
from Burkina Faso, with thanks for your important
work in saving young women from harm

Editor-in-Chief
Bobbie Kalman

Writing team
Bobbie Kalman
Rebecca Sjonger

Substantive editor
Kathryn Smithyman

Project editor
Molly Aloian

Editors
Michael Hodge
Kelley MacAulay

Photo research
Crystal Sikkens

Design
Katherine Berti

Production coordinator
Heather Fitzpatrick

Prepress technician
Nancy Johnson

Consultant
Dr. Michael J. Watts, Professor & Director of African Studies
University of California, Berkley

Illustrations
Barbara Bedell: pages 7 (bird), 16 (rainforest)
Painted by teenage girls in Kongoussi, Burkina Faso, Africa:
     pages 22 (middle), 28 (top), 30 (top left)
Katherine Berti: pages 4 (map), 7 (map), 14 (tree), 19, 21, 24 (map),
     26 (map), 30 (map), 31 (maps)
Robert MacGregor: front cover (map), back cover (map), pages 8-9,
     12 (globe), 14 (map), 16 (map), 18 (map), 20 (map)
Cori Marvin: page 16 (bat)
Vanessa Parson-Robbs: pages 10 (top left), 12 (fish)
Margaret Amy Salter: page 16 (flowers)

Photographs
Bob Burch/Index Stock: page 28 (bottom left)
iStockphoto.com: back cover (bottom), pages 5 (top), 6, 10, 13, 17, 21,
     22 (top), 24, 25, 27 (top), 29 (bottom), 31
Carlos Dominguez/Photo Researchers, Inc.: page 27 (bottom)
Other images by Comstock, Digital Stock, Digital Vision, Iconotec,
     Image Club, Imgram Photo Objects, and Photodisc

Library and Archives Canada Cataloguing in Publication

Kalman, Bobbie, 1947-
     Explore Africa / Bobbie Kalman & Rebecca Sjonger.

(Explore the continents)
Includes index.
ISBN 978-0-7787-3070-5 (bound)
ISBN 978-0-7787-3084-2 (pbk.)

     1. Africa--Geography--Juvenile literature.
I. Sjonger, Rebecca II. Title. III. Series.

DT3.K34 2007   j916   C2007-900725-2

Library of Congress Cataloging-in-Publication Data

Kalman, Bobbie.
     Explore Africa / Bobbie Kalman & Rebecca Sjonger.
       p. cm. -- (Explore the continents)
     Includes index.
     ISBN-13: 978-0-7787-3070-5 (rlb)
     ISBN-10: 0-7787-3070-0 (rlb)
     ISBN-13: 978-0-7787-3084-2 (pb)
     ISBN-10: 0-7787-3084-0 (pb)
     1. Africa--Juvenile literature. 2. Africa--Geography--Juvenile
literature. I. Sjonger, Rebecca. II. Title. III. Series.
     DT3.K215 2007
     916--dc22
                                                        2007003466

Crabtree Publishing Company

Printed in Canada/102017/MA20170906

www.crabtreebooks.com   1-800-387-7650

Published in Canada
Crabtree Publishing
616 Welland Ave.
St. Catharines, ON
L2M 5V6

Published in the United States
Crabtree Publishing
PMB 59051
350 Fifth Avenue, 59th Floor
New York, New York 10118

Published in the United Kingdom
Crabtree Publishing
Maritime House
Basin Road North, Hove
BN41 1WR

Published in Australia
Crabtree Publishing
3 Charles Street
Coburg North
VIC, 3058

Contents

Water and land

Earth is made up of water and land. Water covers almost three-quarters of Earth. The largest areas of water are called **oceans**. There are five oceans on Earth. From largest to smallest, they are the Pacific Ocean, the Atlantic Ocean, the Indian Ocean, the Southern Ocean, and the Arctic Ocean.

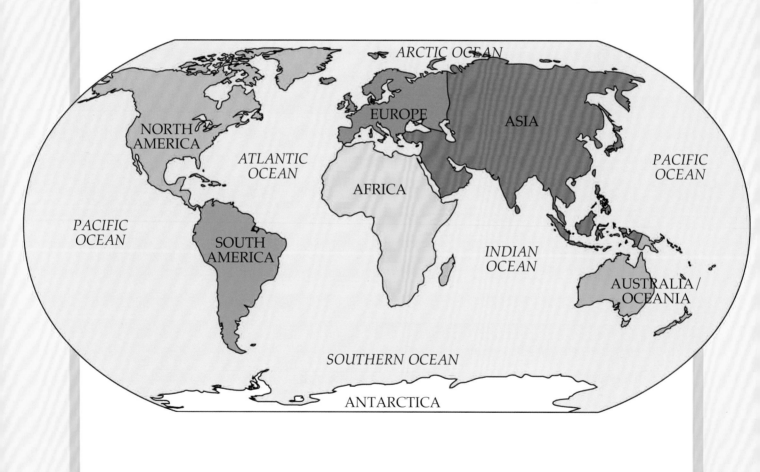

The blue areas on this map show where water is on Earth.

Parts of Africa are close to the Atlantic Ocean.

Huge areas of land

Oceans flow around huge areas of land. These areas of land are called **continents**. There are seven continents on Earth. The continents are Asia, Africa, North America, South America, Antarctica, Europe, and Australia/Oceania.

Tell me about Africa!

Africa is the second-largest continent on Earth. There are 54 **countries** in Africa. A country has **borders** and a **government**. A border is a place where one country ends and another country begins. A government is a group of people who rule a country.

Many animals live in Africa. These cheetahs live in Africa.

WESTERN SAHARA
MOROCCO
TUNISIA
MAURITANIA
SENEGAL
CAPE VERDE
GAMBIA
ALGERIA
LIBYA
EGYPT
MALI
NIGER
CHAD
GUINEA-BISSAU
GUINEA
SIERRA LEONE
LIBERIA
IVORY COAST
BURKINA FASO
GHANA
BENIN
TOGO
NIGERIA
CAMEROON
SAO TOME & PRINCIPE
EQUATORIAL GUINEA
GABON
CONGO
CENTRAL AFRICAN REPUBLIC
DEMOCRATIC REPUBLIC OF THE CONGO
ERITREA
DJIBOUTI
SOMALIA
SUDAN
ETHIOPIA
UGANDA
SEYCHELLES
KENYA
RWANDA
BURUNDI
TANZANIA
COMOROS
ANGOLA
ZAMBIA
BOTSWANA
NAMIBIA
MALAWI
MADAGASCAR
MOZAMBIQUE
SWAZILAND
LESOTHO
ZIMBABWE
SOUTH AFRICA
MAURITIUS

The largest country in Africa is Sudan.

The smallest country in Africa is Seychelles.

Fast fact

There are **islands** in Africa. An island is land that is surrounded by water. Madagascar is the largest island in Africa.

Use the compass

The **compass** on this page shows the four main **directions** on Earth. The four main directions are north, south, east, and west. The letter "N" points north. The **North Pole** is the most northern place on Earth. The letter "S" points south. The most southern point on Earth is the **South Pole**.

NORTH POLE

EQUATOR

SOUTH POLE

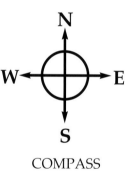

COMPASS

EQUATOR

A line around the center

The **equator** is an imaginary line around the center of Earth. It divides Earth into two equal parts.

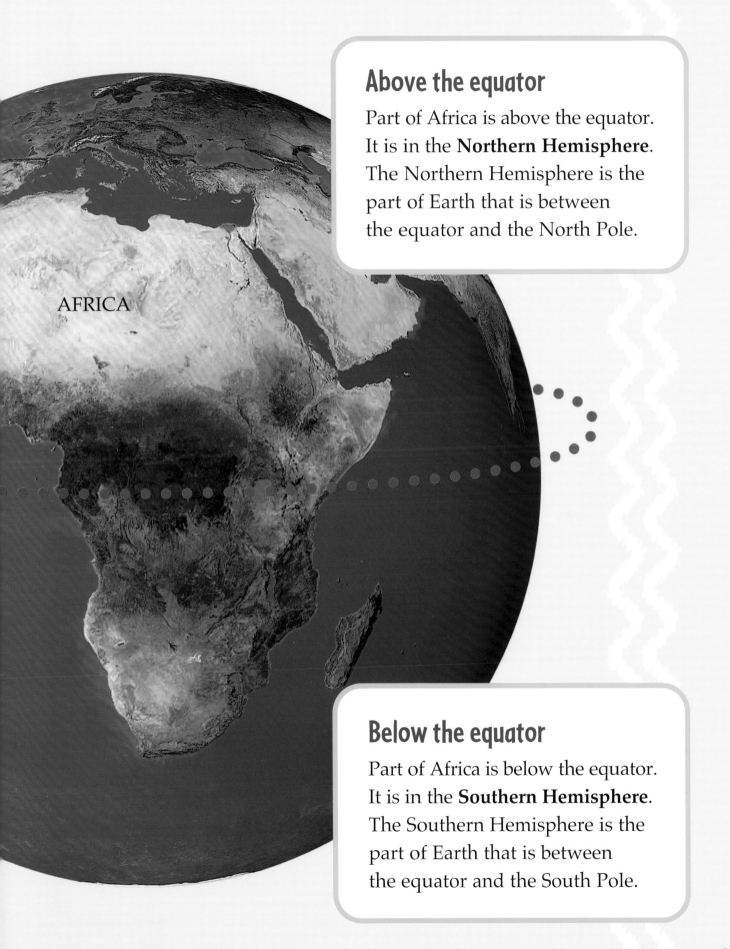

AFRICA

Above the equator

Part of Africa is above the equator. It is in the **Northern Hemisphere**. The Northern Hemisphere is the part of Earth that is between the equator and the North Pole.

Below the equator

Part of Africa is below the equator. It is in the **Southern Hemisphere**. The Southern Hemisphere is the part of Earth that is between the equator and the South Pole.

Hot climate

Near the equator, the **climate** is hot all year long. Climate is the weather in an area over a long period of time. Temperature, rainfall, and wind make up an area's climate. The equator passes through Africa. Most of Africa is hot and sunny all year long. Some parts of Africa have cool weather, however. It is cooler high up on **mountains**.

The weather in Gabon, Uganda, and Kenya is hot all year long. These countries are close to the equator. This mother rhino and her baby live in Kenya. They are resting on a hot afternoon.

Rainy season, dry season

In some parts of Africa, it rains nearly every day. Other places receive almost no rain. There are also areas where it rains part of the year. The rest of the year is dry. The period with rain is called the **rainy season**. The **dry season** is the period when no rain falls.

The country of Senegal has a rainy season. The people who live near water in Senegal build their homes on platforms above the ground. When it rains, the water will not rise high enough to flood their homes.

Waterways

Africa is between two oceans. The Atlantic Ocean is along the west **coast** of Africa. The Indian Ocean is along the east coast of Africa. A coast is an area of land that meets an ocean or a **sea**. A sea is a small part of an ocean with land around it. The northern coast of Africa touches two seas. They are the Red Sea and the Mediterranean Sea.

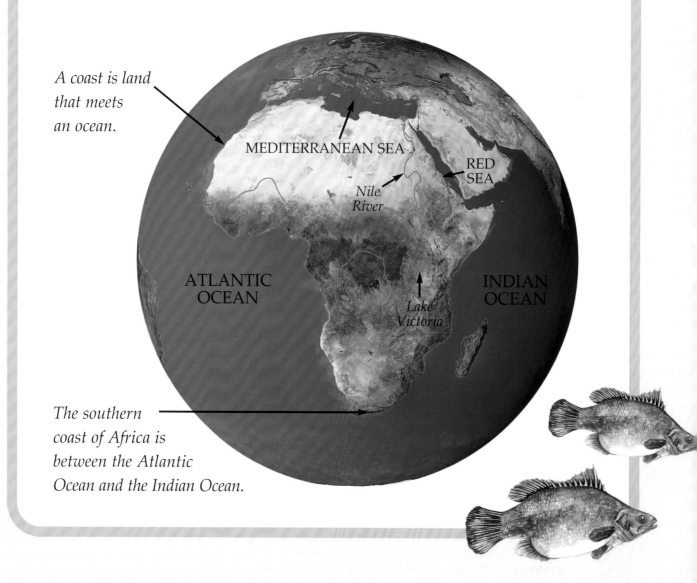

A coast is land that meets an ocean.

MEDITERRANEAN SEA

RED SEA

Nile River

ATLANTIC OCEAN

Lake Victoria

INDIAN OCEAN

The southern coast of Africa is between the Atlantic Ocean and the Indian Ocean.

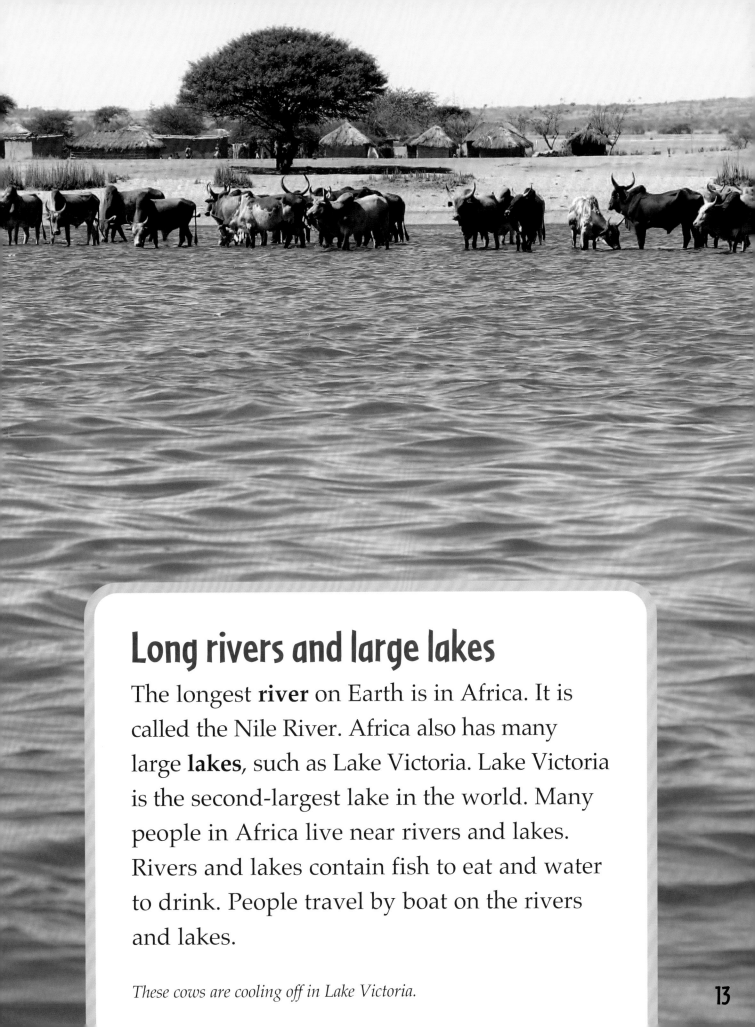

Long rivers and large lakes

The longest **river** on Earth is in Africa. It is called the Nile River. Africa also has many large **lakes**, such as Lake Victoria. Lake Victoria is the second-largest lake in the world. Many people in Africa live near rivers and lakes. Rivers and lakes contain fish to eat and water to drink. People travel by boat on the rivers and lakes.

These cows are cooling off in Lake Victoria.

13

Landforms

There are many tall mountains in Africa. There are also **valleys** in Africa. Valleys are low areas of land between mountains. Mountains and valleys are two kinds of **landforms**. Landforms are areas of land that have different shapes.

Mountains

The weather at the tops of mountains is cold. Some mountaintops even have snow on them! Mount Kilimanjaro is Africa's tallest mountain.

The brown areas on this map show some of the mountains in Africa. The green areas show the Great Rift Valley, which is one of the largest valleys in Africa.

ATLAS MOUNTAINS

AHAGARA MOUNTAINS

TIBESTI MOUNTAINS

RAS DASHEN •

ETHIOPIAN HIGHLANDS

MOUNT STANLEY •

GREAT RIFT VALLEY

MOUNT KENYA •

KILIMANJARO

MOUNT MERU

KATANGA PLATEAU

GREAT KAROO

DRAKENSBERG

mountains   valleys

Valleys

Few people or animals live at the tops of cold mountains. Many people and animals live in valleys, however. Rivers or **streams** often run through valleys. A stream is a small, narrow river. Many plants grow in valleys, too.

This giraffe lives in a valley at the bottom of Mount Kilimanjaro.

Hot, rainy forests

There are **tropical rain forests** in Africa. A tropical rain forest is a kind of forest. Tropical rain forests grow only in places that are hot and rainy.

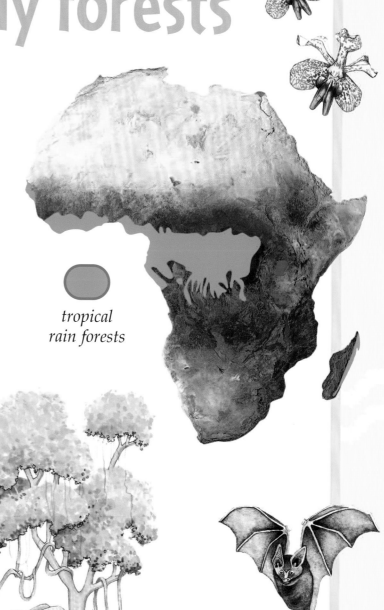

tropical
rain forests

Many kinds of trees grow in the tropical rain forests of Africa. Some of the trees are very tall.

People of the rain forests

Millions of people live in the tropical rain forests of Africa. Some people hunt animals and gather plants in the forests. They hunt and gather to find food to eat. Other people are farmers.

These boys live near a tropical rain forest. They are collecting firewood for cooking.

Fast fact

Many animals live high in the trees of tropical rain forests. Bats, birds, and monkeys live high in trees.

Grasslands

There are many **grasslands** in Africa. Grasslands are large areas of land that are covered in grasses. African grasslands are called **savannas**. Bushes and some types of trees, such as acacia trees, grow on savannas. Africa's largest animals live on savannas. Elephants, hippopotamuses, and rhinoceroses are big animals. Giraffes, antelopes, zebras, lions, cheetahs, and leopards are other savanna animals.

grasslands

Elephants are huge savanna animals. They eat a lot of grasses.

People on savannas

Many people also live on African savannas. They grow **crops** on parts of these grasslands. Crops are plants that are grown for food. People also raise **livestock** such as cows. Livestock eat the plants that grow on savannas.

This Maasai man raises cows on a grassland area.

Sandy deserts

There are huge **deserts** in Africa. Deserts are very hot, dry areas. Deserts receive less than 10 inches (25 cm) of rain each year. The **soil** in many African deserts is sandy. Strong winds blow the sand. The winds blow the sand into large hills called **sand dunes**.

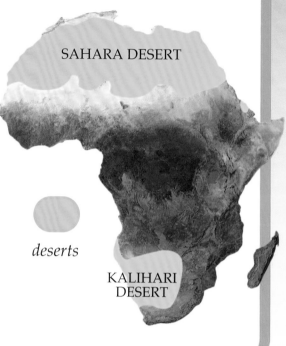

SAHARA DESERT

deserts

KALIHARI DESERT

Fast fact

The Sahara Desert is the largest desert in the world. This big desert is about the same size as the whole area of the United States!

Few living things

Animals need water to stay alive. There is very little water in deserts. Most animals cannot survive there, but camels, snakes, and scorpions can. These animals do not need to drink a lot of water to stay alive.

African snake

*Some people live in African deserts. They are called **nomads**. Nomads travel from place to place looking for water to drink and food to eat. They also need to find water and food for their animals.*

Rural areas

More than 800 million people live in Africa! Many Africans live in **rural areas**. A rural area is a place outside of a city or a town. Many people who live in rural areas live in **villages**. They build their own homes. They find food on the land or in waterways near their homes.

This boy is carrying chickens home to his family.

Farming to survive

Africans who live in the countryside may be far from stores, schools, and hospitals. Many people in rural areas are farmers. They grow their own food to eat. They grow food crops such as corn, yams, and **millet**. They may also own some livestock, such as cows or sheep.

These women are pounding millet to make it into flour.

People die every day

Many Africans die every day from **diseases** such as **AIDS** and **malaria**. Most do not have enough money to buy the medicines they need. Also, there are very few doctors to help them get well. Other people die because they do not have clean water to drink.

Urban areas

Cities and towns are **urban areas**. African cities are like other cities around the world. They have tall buildings and many roads filled with cars. The picture above shows Cape Town. This big city is in South Africa.

This map shows some large cities in Africa.

CASABLANCA
TUNIS
CAIRO
LAGOS
ABIDJAN
NAIROBI
KINSHASA
JOHANNESBURG
CAPE TOWN

Very little money

Almost half of all African people live in urban areas. Many of these people live in very poor conditions. Some people do not have jobs. People who do have jobs often have very little money. Most people live in simple homes or shacks.

*The parts of cities where people live in shacks are called **slums**.*

Useful materials

Every continent has **natural resources**. A natural resource is a material found in nature that people can use. Natural resources make money for African countries. People can buy and sell natural resources inside and outside Africa. **Minerals** such as oil and diamonds are some of Africa's most important natural resources. Many people work for companies that buy and sell natural resources.

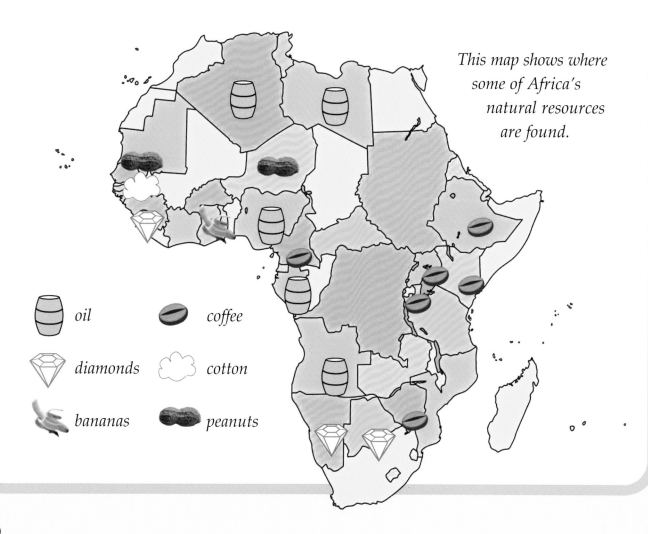

This map shows where some of Africa's natural resources are found.

oil

diamonds

bananas

coffee

cotton

peanuts

Grown to be sold

Some natural resources are **cash crops**. Cash crops are crops that people grow so they can sell them. Some African farmers grow cash crops on small farms. Large companies grow cash crops on big farms called **plantations**. Cotton, bananas, and coffee are three kinds of cash crops.

People all over the world enjoy foods that come from Africa.

These men have gathered beans that grow on coffee plants in Zimbabwe. The beans are dried and then roasted. People use the beans to make coffee.

African culture

Culture is the beliefs, customs, and ways of life that a group of people share. People create art, music, and dances to **express**, or show, their cultures. Activities such as sports and games are also parts of many cultures. These pages show some of the ways in which African people express their cultures.

Sculpture

People around the world love African **sculptures**. Sculptures are kinds of art. People make sculptures by carving or shaping them. They make sculptures from materials such as wood, stone, metal, and clay.

This artist is carving a sculpture.

Music

Music is a part of everyday life in Africa. Music is also part of many **celebrations**. Most African music includes drumming.

This is an African drum.

Dance

In Africa, listening to music often leads to dancing! Some dancing is just for fun. People also perform certain dances to celebrate events in their lives such as weddings or religious festivals. This African dancer is performing a dance that is an important part of his culture. He performs the dance wearing a mask and a special costume.

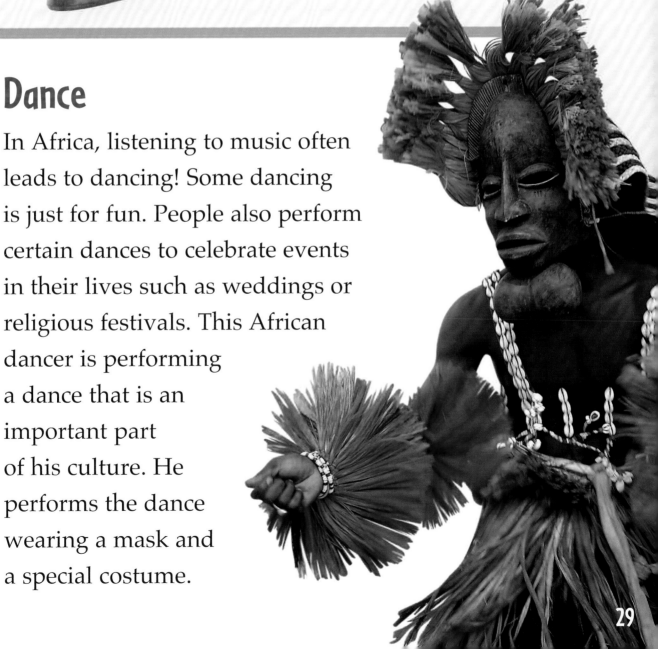

Postcards from Africa

Africa is a beautiful continent. People from all over the world visit Africa to see the land and the many wild animals. They also visit to learn about African cultures. Here are some places and things that many people come to see. The maps on these pages show where they can be found in Africa.

The Sphinx is in Egypt. It is a huge stone figure of a person's head on a lion's body. It was carved over 4,500 years ago.

Victoria Falls is one of the tallest waterfalls in the world. It is on the border between Zambia and Zimbabwe.

*This ranger works at a **preserve** in Africa. Many people visit Kenya, Tanzania, Uganda, and Zimbabwe to learn about helping animals in the wild.*

Glossary

Note: Boldfaced words that are defined in the text may not appear in the glossary.

AIDS **A**cquired **I**mmune **D**eficiency **S**yndrome—a deadly illness that attacks the body's ability to protect itself from other illnesses

celebration A ceremony held for an event or on a special day

disease An illness that makes people sick

lake A large area of water that is surrounded by land

livestock Animals, such as cows, which people raise for food

malaria A deadly disease that causes a very high fever and chills

millet A cereal plant that can be made into flour

minerals Substances, such as coal and gold, that people remove from the ground

mountain An area of high land that has steep sides

preserve A place where wildlife is protected

river A large area of water that flows into an ocean, a lake, or another river

soil The upper layer of earth

tropical rain forest A hot, thick forest that receives at least 100 inches (254 cm) of rain each year

village A group of houses in a rural area

Index